Contents

Personal stories: 'Brown Bear and Wilbur Wolf'

Brown Bear was hungry. He had been asleep all winter. He came out of his den and stretched. The snow had melted and the grass was green. Brown Bear looked around him and sniffed the air, but he couldn't smell anything.

He went into the forest to look for berries, but he couldn't smell anything.

He went to the river to look for fish, but he couldn't smell anything.

'I've lost my smell,' he said sadly to himself. 'How will I find any food?'

He lay down in a meadow by the river and tried to remember all his favourite smells — the smell of trees, the smell of new grass, the smell of apples and leaves, of berries, of rain and snow.

Get started

Draw pictures of the things that
Brown Bear remembered and label them.

1. the trees and grass

2. the apples and leaves

3. the berries

4. the rain and snow

Try these

Copy and complete the sentences using your own ideas.

1. Brown Bear felt …

2. The weather was …

3. Brown Bear went to …

4. The problem was …

Now try these

1. What is Brown Bear thinking about at the end
of the story? Write a sentence.

2. Draw a picture of Brown Bear looking sad
or worried. Add a caption.

3. What happens next? Write the next part of
the story.

4. Plan a short story about a character looking for
something they have lost.

Fairy tale: 'Puss in Boots'

Once upon a time, in a windmill on top of a hill, there lived an old man and his three sons. When the old man died,
he left the windmill to the eldest son, a donkey to the second and a cat called Puss to the third.

The youngest son was upset. He wanted to have the windmill or the donkey. 'I am fond of you, Puss,' he said, as he stroked the cat, 'but you're not very useful. Except for catching mice!'

Get started

Copy the sentences and complete them using words from the fairy tale.

1. Once upon a time, there was a
_____ on top of a hill.

2. In the _____ there lived an
_____ _____ and his
three sons.

3. The eldest son was given the _____ .

4. The second son was given a _____ .

5. The youngest son was given a _____ .

Try these

Write the next part of the fairy tale by copying and completing the sentences.

1. The youngest son went to live in …

2. He got a job as …

3. The cat stayed with him and they …

4. One day he was asked to give the cat to …

5. Then an amazing thing happened …

Now try these

1. Draw a picture of the third son looking disappointed about getting the cat.

2. Write a sentence to explain how the son felt about Puss.

3. What are the son and Puss saying in your picture? Add speech bubbles to your picture.

4. Plan your own story about Puss. Draw and label pictures or write a few sentences.

Traditional tale: 'The Fox and the Crow'

'How delicious!' thought Crow, looking at a picnic left lying in the shade. 'So much food ... And no one's around ...'

Her beady black eye was caught by a piece of juicy meat lying just out of reach. 'Oh!' thought Crow. 'It's so tempting. If I swoop down fast enough,' she decided, 'I can get it, I'm sure.'

And she went for it, darting down, a blur of black feathers. Snap, snap, went her sharp beak, and then she headed back into the woods, flapping her fringed wings, a very proud thief.

Get started

Copy the sentences and complete them using words for different kinds of food.

1. 'How delicious! I can see _____ ,' thought Crow.

2. 'Oh yum! I can smell _____ ,' said Crow.

3. 'Wow! There's _____ ,' exclaimed Crow.

4. 'Scrumptious! A big juicy _____ ,' declared Crow.

5. 'That _____ looks tasty!' cackled Crow.

Try these

Answer the questions to create a story opening for 'The Fox and the Crow'.

1. When did the story happen?

2. Where did the story happen?

3. What was the weather like in the story?

4. What time was it in the story?

5. Who was there at the start of the story?

Now try these

1. Write a sentence about Crow taking some more food.

2. Think of a new animal character. Draw a picture of them talking to Crow.

3. What are they saying? Add speech bubbles to your picture.

4. Plan your own short story about an animal that takes some food. Draw and label a picture or write some sentences.

Information writing: Volcano danger

Vesuvius began to erupt in AD 79. A mighty earthquake shook the ground. Clouds of ash hid the sun and the sky went dark. The people of Pompeii were terrified.

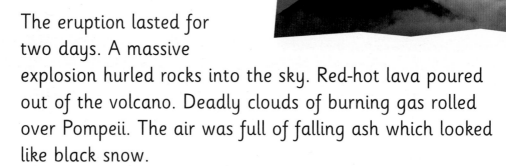

The eruption lasted for two days. A massive explosion hurled rocks into the sky. Red-hot lava poured out of the volcano. Deadly clouds of burning gas rolled over Pompeii. The air was full of falling ash which looked like black snow.

Get started

Copy the sentences and decide if they are facts or opinions. Then write 'fact' or 'opinion'.

1. Vesuvius began to erupt in AD 79.

2. I think it was noisy.

3. I think it was very scary.

4. The eruption lasted for two days.

5. The explosion hurled rocks into the sky.

Try these

Read the text and write a sentence to answer each question.

1. What is the text about?

2. What is the first fact in the text?

3. What was the first thing that happened when Vesuvius erupted?

4. How long did the eruption last?

5. How many sentences are there in the text?

Now try these

1. Draw a picture of Vesuvius erupting. Label the different parts of your picture.

2. Draw a picture of the people of Pompeii watching Vesuvius erupt.

3. What are the people of Pompeii saying? Add speech bubbles to your picture.

4. Plan ideas for an information text about your school. Draw and label a picture or write some sentences.

Report: Ancient Egyptians

The Ancient Egyptians were farmers who lived along the banks of the Nile. They used water from the river to help them grow food. The Egyptians were ruled by a powerful king called a pharaoh.

Pharaohs and pyramids

Some pharaohs were buried inside huge, stone pyramids on the edge of the desert. The pharaoh's body was placed in a secret room in the middle of the pyramid.

Get started

Copy the sentences and decide if they are true or false. Then write 'true' or 'false'.

1. Reports can use headings.

2. Reports can use topic-specific words.

3. Reports are always about Ancient Egypt.

4. Reports need very long sentences.

5. Reports never use full sentences.

Try these

Read the report and answer the questions.

1. What is the report about?

2. There are two headings. What are they?

3. Who were the Ancient Egyptians?

4. What does the second section of the report focus on?

5. Find three facts. Write them down.

Now try these

1. Draw a picture of the Ancient Egyptians building a pyramid. Label your picture.

2. What else would you like to know about the Ancient Egyptians? Write a heading for a third section of the report.

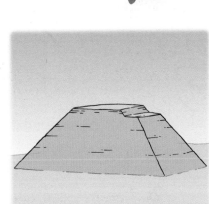

3. Write five key words for a report on Ancient Egypt.

4. Plan ideas for a report on a topic you have been learning about in school. Draw and label a picture or write some sentences.

Simple instructions: Papier maché house

You will need lots of newspaper, a small cardboard box, a fork, a bowl, one cup of flour, one and a half cups of water, a teaspoon of salt, and a quarter of a cup of white glue.

Clear a large area and cover the table with newspaper. Put the water and the flour into the bowl, and mix together with the fork until it is runny. Mix in the salt and the glue. Tear newspaper into strips. Dip a strip completely into the paste, then remove excess paste by running the strip between your thumb and finger. Lay the strip on the cardboard box. Do the same with more strips until the box is completely covered. Leave the box to dry, then cover it again with new strips. Let it dry again and cover it one more time with strips. Then your house is ready for painting!

Get started

Copy and complete the instructions using your own imperative (bossy) verbs.

1. _____ the things you will need.

2. _____ your hands.

3. _____ the items on the table.

4. _____ the instructions carefully.

5. _____ the table afterwards.

Try these

Write one instruction for part of each task.

1. washing hands

2. getting dressed

3. making breakfast

4. making a birthday card

5. going to bed

Now try these

1. What do we call the bossy verbs that are used in instructions?

2. Draw and label a diagram to show how to tidy up a mess.

3. Draw and label a diagram to show how to peel an orange.

4. Write your own set of instructions to explain how to do one of the following:

   • dance the hokeycokey

   • make a paper aeroplane

   • draw an animal (you choose what animal)

Simple explanations: How does a kite work?

Kites come in many shapes and sizes, but they all use the wind to fly.

A kite is a frame covered in light material. It has a thin, strong piece of string tied to the frame. As you hold up a kite, air lifts it up so that it can fly.

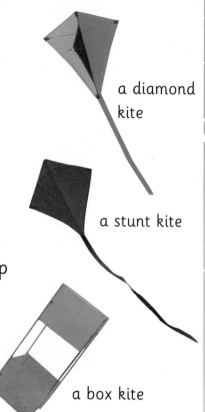

a diamond kite

a stunt kite

a box kite

Get started

Copy the sentences and decide if they are true or false. Then write 'true' or 'false'.

1. All kites are diamond shaped.

2. All kites are blue.

3. Kites come in many shapes and sizes.

4. Only some kites use the wind to fly.

5. Kites have a frame covered in light material.

Try these

Copy and complete the sentences using your own ideas.

1. A kite is a …

2. It is best to fly a kite when …

3. If you are in a busy park, …

4. Your string might …

5. Flying a kite is …

Now try these

1. Draw and label a diagram of a kite.

2. Write a sentence to explain what a pencil is.

3. Write a sentence to explain what a book is.

4. Write a short explanation to help people understand what a bicycle is and how to ride it.

Word play: 'My Name Is ...'

My name is Sluggery-wuggery
My name is Worms-for-tea
My name is Swallow-the-table-leg
My name is Drink-the-sea.
My name is I-eat-saucepans
My name is I-like-snails
My name is Grand-piano-George
My name is I-ride-whales.
My name is Jump-the-chimney
My name is Bite-my-knee
My name is Jiggery-pokery
And Riddle-me-ree,
and ME.

Pauline Clarke

Get started

Copy the sentences and decide if they are true or false.
Then write 'true' or 'false'.

1. The poem repeats the words 'My name is'.

2. The poem uses hyphens to join words together.

3. The poem uses some made-up words.

4. The poem is thirteen lines long.

5. The poem does not rhyme.

Try these

Copy and complete the phrases using your own words.

1. My name is _____ window

2. My name is _____ paper

3. My name is _____ handbag

4. My name is _____ spiders

5. My name is _____ centipede

Now try these

1. What do you think Sluggery-wuggery looks like? Draw a picture.

2. What would you say to Sluggery-wuggery if you met him?

3. Write two silly sentences that start with 'My age is ...'.

4. Write your own silly poem. Start each line of your poem with 'My toys are ...'.

Poetry: 'Don't Call Alligator Long-Mouth till You Cross River'

Call alligator long-mouth

call alligator saw-mouth

call alligator pushy-mouth

call alligator scissors-mouth

call alligator raggedy-mouth

call alligator bumpy-bum

call alligator all dem rude word

but better wait

till you cross river.

John Agard

Get started

Copy the sentences and decide if they are true or false.
Then write 'true' or 'false'.

1. The poem is about a chimpanzee.

2. The poem repeats the words 'call alligator'.

3. 'dem' is a mistake made by the poet.

4. 'dem' shows the poet speaks with an accent.

5. All of the insults are about the alligator's eyes.

Try these

Copy the phrases and complete them using words for different
kinds of animal.

1. call _____ wide-mouth

2. call _____ short-legs

3. call _____ razor-claws

4. call _____ wobble-nose

5. call _____ messy-paws

Now try these

1. Draw and label a picture of the alligator.

2. What might the alligator say? Add a speech bubble to your picture.

3. Write two 'call alligator' sentences that are nice rather than insulting.

4. Write your own fun poem about a different animal using the style of 'Don't Call Alligator Long-Mouth till You Cross River'